D1579366

THERE'S A STEGOSAURUS ON THE STAIRS

Aleksei Bitskoff & Ruth Symons

QED

QED Publishing

Stegosaurus was a large plant-eating dinosaur with a row of bony

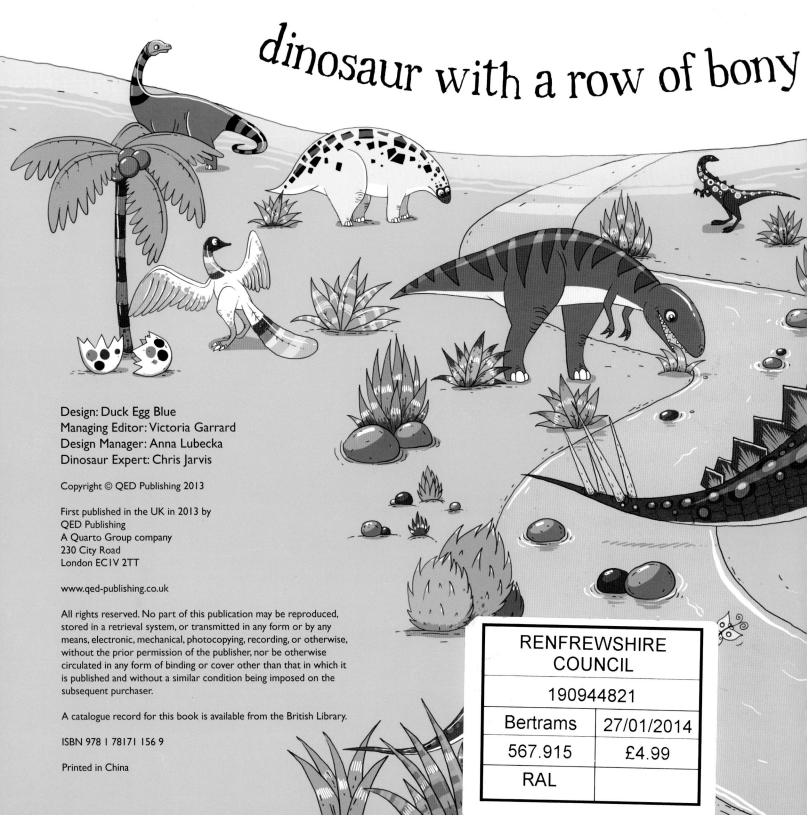

Design: Duck Egg Blue
Managing Editor: Victoria Garrard
Design Manager: Anna Lubecka
Dinosaur Expert: Chris Jarvis

Copyright © QED Publishing 2013

First published in the UK in 2013 by
QED Publishing
A Quarto Group company
230 City Road
London EC1V 2TT

www.qed-publishing.co.uk

All rights reserved. No part of this publication may be reproduced,
stored in a retrieval system, or transmitted in any form or by any
means, electronic, mechanical, photocopying, recording, or otherwise,
without the prior permission of the publisher, nor be otherwise
circulated in any form of binding or cover other than that in which it
is published and without a similar condition being imposed on the
subsequent purchaser.

A catalogue record for this book is available from the British Library.

ISBN 978 1 78171 156 9

Printed in China

RENFREWSHIRE COUNCIL	
190944821	
Bertrams	27/01/2014
567.915	£4.99
RAL	

plates running down his back.

He lived around **150 million** years ago – many millions of years before the first humans appeared.

But just imagine if Stegosaurus was alive today! How would he cope with modern life?

What if Stegosaurus went to the playground?

Stegosaurus would need a big friend to balance him on the see-saw. He weighed nearly 5 tonnes – that's as much as an elephant!

He might not keep up in class.
His brain was only the
size of a tangerine!

What if Stegosaurus went on a school trip?

Stegosaurus would **always** stick with the group. Stegosaurus families lived in big herds, which kept them safe from predators.

So Stegosaurus knows it's **not safe** to wander off!

What if Stegosaurus went for a walk?

He wouldn't fit on the pavement. At 9 metres long and 2 metres wide he's as...

BIG as a bus!

If he walked in the road he'd cause a traffic jam. He could only walk at 8 or 9 kilometres per hour – that's not much faster than you.

What if Stegosaurus went to a party?

He could use his big, spiky tail to burst the piñata and get all the sweets!

Stegosaurus had four big

spikes

on his tail. Each spike was as long as your arm.

And the jelly would really **wobble** when he started dancing.

Stegosaurus would weigh more than the rest of the party put together!

What would Stegosaurus give his mum on mother's day?

Stegosaurus could use his
sharp beak
to cut her a bunch of flowers.

His beak was **perfect** for snipping plant stems to...

munch on!

What if Stegosaurus sat on a whoopee cushion?

Pffffffffffffffffffffffffffffft!

He'd be so embarrassed he would blush – but not in his cheeks!

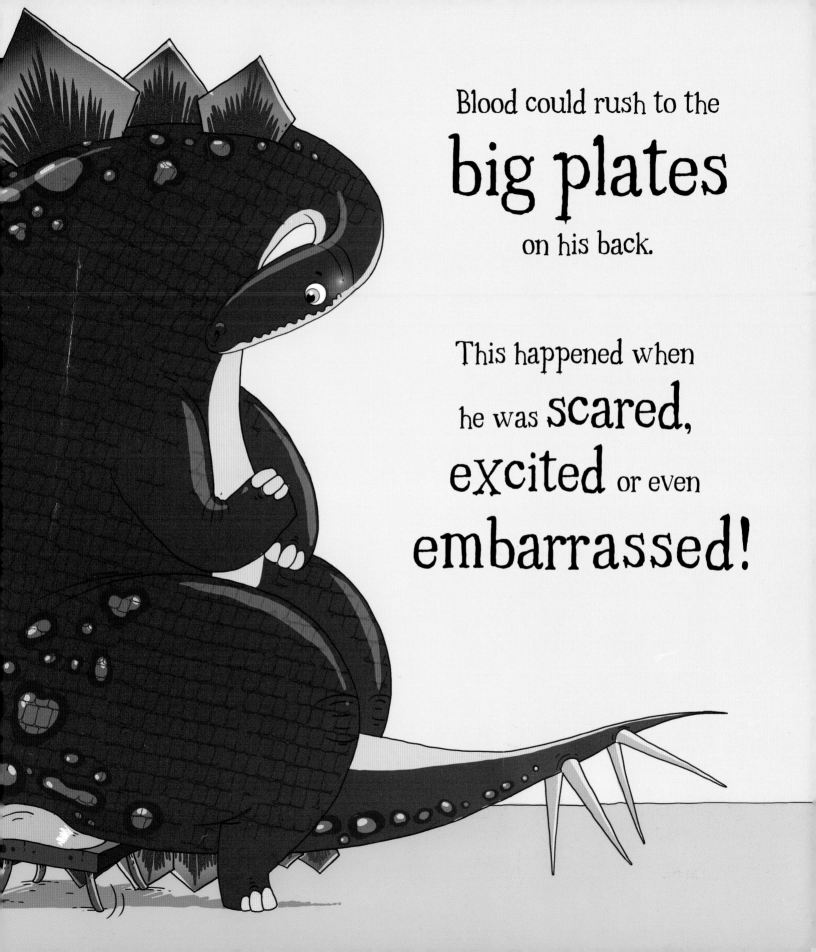

Blood could rush to the **big plates** on his back.

This happened when he was **scared**, **excited** or even **embarrassed!**

What if Stegosaurus went to the supermarket?

He could sniff out the ripest, yummiest fruit.

Stegosaurus had an **amazing** sense of smell... much better than his eyesight!

What if Stegosaurus was sleepy?

Stegosaurus would probably sleep curled on his side, like elephants and other large animals do today.

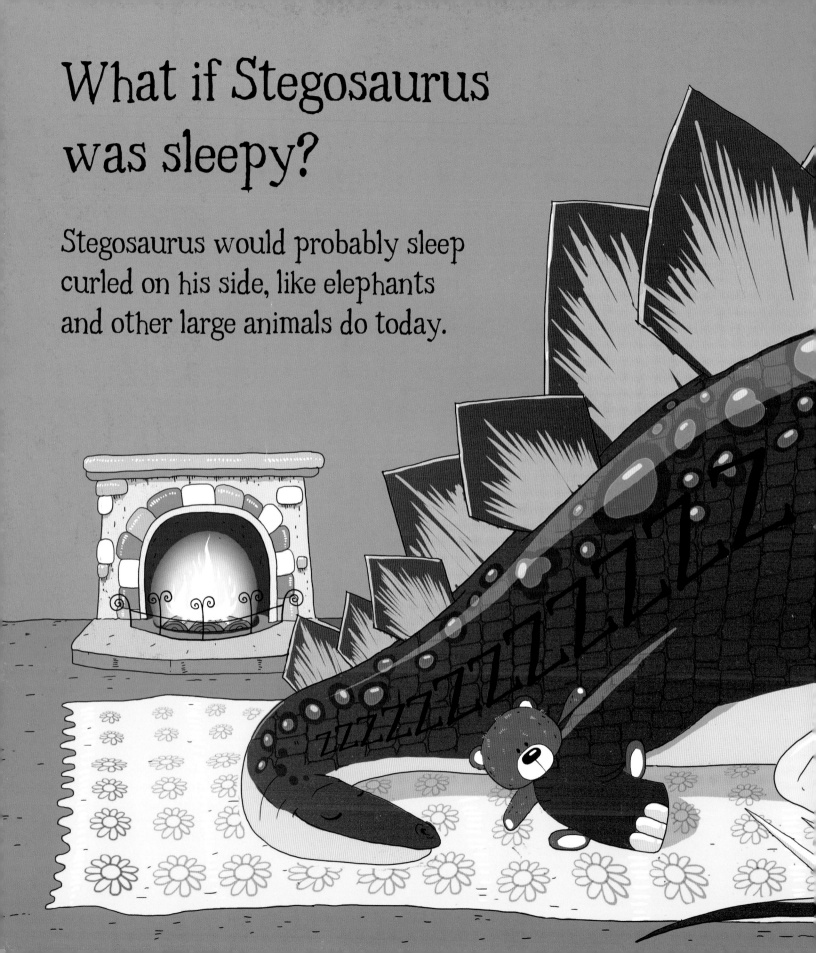

He might also be able to doze
while standing on all fours,
like rhinos, horses and
other animals still do.

Stegosaurus's skeleton

Everything we know about Stegosaurus comes from fossils – skeletons that have been in the ground for thousands and thousands of years.

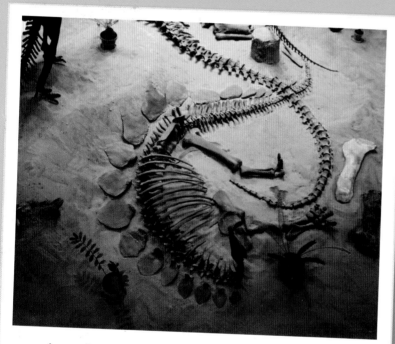

Scientists can look at fossils to work out how dinosaurs lived in the past.

This means we know lots about dinosaurs, even though no one has ever seen one!

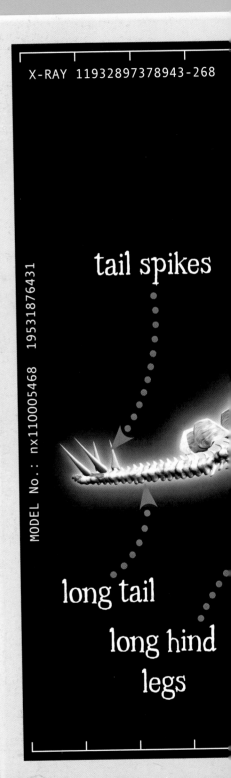

X-RAY 11932897378943-268

MODEL No.: nx110005468 19531876431

tail spikes

long tail

long hind legs

bony plates

sharp beak

small skull

short front legs

COLORADO, USA
Most complete skeleton discovered, nicknamed 'Spike' – 1992

AUSTRALIA
Fossil footprints discovered – 1995

WYOMING, USA
Back plates discovered – 1879

PORTUGAL
Partial skeleton discovered – 2006

UTAH, USA
Fossil remains found – 2010

COLORADO, USA
First skeleton found – 1876

PASSPORT

Stegosaurus

(STEG-OH-SORE-US)

NAME MEANS 'ROOF LIZARD' SCIENTISTS ONCE THOUGHT HIS BACK PLATES LAY FLAT, LIKE ROOF TILES.

WEIGHT 5 TONNES

LENGTH 9 METRES

HEIGHT 3 METRES

HABITAT WOODS, FOREST

DIET FERNS, LEAVES, PINE NEEDLES

2340712098987246435

S<STEG<<STEGOSAURUS<<<<<<<<<<<<34263954302375<<<<<<<<<<48273526291083546>>>>>>>>